The Sumptuous Hills of Gulfport

The Sumptuous Hills of Gulfport

Vincent Spina

ISBN: 978-1-942956-49-5
Library of Congress Control Number: 2017961047

Cover Photo: Bruno Minkley

Lamar University Literary Press
Beaumont, Texas

Acknowledgments

I am grateful to the editors of the following publications, where some of the poems in this collection originally appeared:

Fell Swoop
The Bridge Literary Arts Journal
Voices de la luna

The symbolism of "Mayan Tongues" and "'Aya Uma'Spirit Mask" comes from my own times living among the Native People, the Runacuna of Otavalo, Ecuador.

I am deeply indebted to my friend Roberto Bonazzi for his comments and advice as I labored through writing and placing these poems in some kind of order. I also thank Kay Fineran Luthin for her comments and encouragement. Finally, thanks to Ellen Noto, my partner, who keeps it all honest and heartfelt.

Recent Poetry from Lamar University Literary Press

For
Ellen Noto

CONTENTS

Boca Ciega: Late April

And one day
        nothing has changed
—the tiny bay and its homeless
        sloops and the condo-laden
islands beyond—

yet the black skimmers are
        not there
hunkered down in the white sand
        their red and black beaks
        —clown beaks, misshapen
scissors pointed into the wind—

deadly, as they—the night flyers
        the silent flyers—
skim the surface of the dusk-becalmed bay
        for the right fish in the wrong place
        at the wrong time.

A need has pressed them—mechanical
        like the turning of a small planet
        around its axis, as it
        orbits a distant sun.
And there

on Cape May with its dressing of seasonal amusements
        and motels
at Lewes and the hidden stretches
        of the Delaware shore
on a small island off the coast of Long Island

they appear
in the sand, clown beaks once more
        turned into the wind
as if nothing had changed
        —Had they ever left?—

the long flight, forgotten,
the lost ones over the Atlantic and
over Virginia and Maryland corn fields
      freshly sprouting back to life
—no longer a memory.

Only the need
      —from winter to summer grounds—
twines about the hub of their existence:

thread through an expanding fabric
      as they return to nest
      nourish the new season of hatchlings
      until they fledge
—union

of male and female: union
of what is the male and what the female:
a tenderness

that now binds—intimation of love
      before the notion
      before the word—

Amoeba, mammal, plant, bird
      reptile, fish
double helix:

A revolution. Mix it all together.
      No matter.
We are all involved.

Inland Waterway

It's a short dream, but a happy dream.
— *Kiss of the Spider Woman*, Manuel Puig

The way a tree grows
without compunction or conscious purpose:

a sudden traffic jam as you cross a bridge
that didn't mean to take you anywhere
as right now you mean not
to be anywhere.

What is the name for tide?
or the way her hip moved with the grace
of a wave
or even an ocean? Sometimes

it is a caring bench
on the side of a path through palmettos
that counts. Otherwise,
who'd be watching your back. Yet

I am so glad you've given up
on smoking. How long has it been
...two minutes, twenty years?

This year the eggs are ready.
Make that two for me, please, with bacon
or those tiny bits of sausage that float
into memories of those Saturdays
before Easter.

I'm as hungry as a kayak
drifting on the Inland Waterway.

The Gran Cesar

The immense pink castle-cum-hotel
shimmers on her shoestring stretch of sand,
dolls-or-"Dalís" up the mist drifting in on kitten paws
from the Gulf of these special occasions,

begging the question
of the Broken Easter Egg and
its subsequent effects on Western well-being
—but, please, no Humpty-Dumpty
falls here, as season follows
season, follow seasons. We are

here, lying in the sun, half hormones,
half refugees, half lotus flowers.
"Who's out there?" she asks, lifting
her head from her beach towel to count
the flowers on her bikini, hear more cleanly
the raps, the cumbias, the salsas,
the forgiveness and the tomorrows. We are

all here these F. Scott Fitzgerald days
—Long Island Gold Coast flown South
and painted pink in homage
to the good times barely remembered
we fondly remember, filling the gaps
with each one's good intentions,

as young men, wearing their sun-drenched
muscles, answer her calls, and children
glide past on their Ferris wheels,
balanced high up on this point
our whole lives have been aiming for.

A Day Without a Poem

is like a prison camp without an ocean
to long for. Once a vagrant sloop
approached me on the wooden pier at Boca Ciega.

Index
missing on his left hand, gash of ecstasy
in joy and mourning cut in the palm of his right. Freely,
he gave me the time of day—skimmer tuned and pelican
distant as dolphins roll on cue forever to fix
and feast the mind on. The yawls were all bounding for somewhere
—whiskey night still vapid on the breath of dawn.

Yes, traveler, anywhere
is here. You can't help being at the center. She
is like a cat who follows you everywhere
more intimately than your shadow.
Was I talking to myself?

To whom else, replied the hobby horse,
would this obsession be talking to, on this fantastic,
phantasmagoric "Lupe-d'-loop" spuming
from my tongue to the page?

In the drop-dead, dreadnaught maw of things
infested with sadness, desire and awe of things
we sit encapsulated—moth and flutter of sail
born in the breeze and bears the breeze
to the mouth of blind bay (though in the end
all bays must be blind).

Am I then supposed to draw a fine line between
the hills, entwining runnels and the sea?

Dreamt Poem

Only one thing remained reachable, close and secure amid all
losses: language
— Paul Celan

I

Far fetched and nothing certain, he
may have been a cook from a rice growing community
        or whaling village on the coast
of a lesser island in the waters of the nearby mainland,

though he had no specialty and the morphing
patterns of his speech—then and there—predicted
the food he was preparing
        which became his specialty. Flamencos danced

as he cooked over open fires mussels and shrimps
        of the southern rices; zampognas
droned the birth of a god or spider dance
as he baked the pignole and raisin cakes
        that promised eternal life
to small towns at the eastern edge of a salty sea.

Gradually he changed as, neck deep
in trenches of horror and despair, he brewed
the healing stews that brought pleasant dreams
to countless women grieving their children
who now enriched the soils of ceaseless fields of bone
        —he was the dancer,
        mother to mothers.

But the need was great.
He could not keep up.
No one could...only the peace
of words that follows
the bottomless grief.

II

He was pursued
by saints and assassins.
He could not keep up:

anonymous cook in New York's China town
shaking a wok in a steamy autumn kitchen,
brandishing a wooden spoon in the face
of hidden crocodiles;

mountain goddess
festooned in Alpine blossoms, hair
      descending like uphill rivers
to nourish the field of people who,
      dark in their dreams,
still longed and with mirrors lured
      her from her cave,

who made from her flesh the white
and yellow corn tortillas to feed
a town iced in time,

who was seen picking apples
in an apple orchard
growing plum tomatoes
in a small garden
watching grand and great-grand children play
as she rocked in a hammock issued
      during World War I or II.

The need was great.
He could not keep up.

Palm

If a palm tree dies in the middle of a swamp
and all the anoles who've come to mourn
perish mid-stream, will I still be gazing
at the moon but seeing you, just

returning from the beach toting
your blue and yellow pail you've
just filled with an entire summer's worth
of warm gulf water—you who are to you

as a child is to the castle she builds
in the sand, and who forgives me this digression
into the popular, the clichés, and, otherwise,
banal? My, how you have grown, with

your scented handkerchief of fine Irish linen
bordered in green lace, now on display
in the window of one of those fancy vanity shops
just off Fifth Avenue (Mannahatta, city without Lenni

Lenape) and how the world in real life and memory too
grows around us like a budding grove, until
we hardly remember if we fit anymore
but we do, as you slip into

something more comfortable, only to sit down
to your memoirs—fiction or real? Yet,
isn't it always a fiction and real, a poem: how I
saved you from the train wreck, only

much later to realize it was you who'd saved me?
Is it the ache in the teeth, the breasts that go
missing their twins? All these things count, slowly
sometimes, like the subtext of a long novel

which suddenly becomes, more urgent
than the main character and his or her

many strifes, and all this, as the dim
light overhead diminishes further

and the image of your self, which you
had been studying through the glass
pane of the subway window, disappears
and the true-you of the novel is now there

in the tunnel's darkness which is
no longer dark since you, for that one moment,
are no longer dark, but a traveler
content with her body, but glad to escape

from time to time, book passage
on a steamer to this nowhere in particular
of a dream as in the song or poem, but can't
because body is to soul as soul is to body.

My, how you have grown. The blue and yellow
pail too—if only...if only so many times and things
and places to go and people lying on beaches
as always. As always.

The MFA in St. Petersburg

> ...sometimes I think I'm "in love" with painting,
> — Frank O'Hara

Fifteen dollars. Steep price
     and "senior admission" no less...
(sometimes I think...) then
the sudden rush of cold air
     is shocking at first, but nice
     on the surface of moist skin

yet outside you'd hardly want to leave
     those immense Banyans
     magic triumphant stranglers like
     an unfinished dream in the head
     of Gaudí.

And the harbor
I never know if they are ketches or yawls
but the yachts. yacht after yacht
     by the billions of dollars of yachts
while children wash up on shores
dying at every conceivable border yet
     life is also conceivable, and nourishment
     and beauty is conceivable. I hate

the guided tours from painting to painting
     —I can never do (as "in love") more
     than five of six   the rest
is a restless chaos of colors flowing into colors
     and not wanting to be there anymore
     like getting dressed, putting on your shoes
     after bad sex

Today by myself, enough will be enough.

I bypass the first gallery (Bronzes
     from Tibet and Nepal)

open on to a gallery of modern and
contemporary works:
"Black Watch": Gene Davis, 1974
(Mondrian influence?) a series of differently colored vertical
       lines running the length of the painting: "If you fix
your eyes on one color and follow the lines of the same color
horizontally across the page, you'll get
what I'm aiming at," but I get dizzy
       and can't stop dancing.

And "Dancing in the Street": Mary L. Procter, 1996
studded with spangles and gold chains
       buttons and photos (of Mary?)
Primitive artist...on flat boards
       and doors. A sudden epiphany
       in the old sense of the word. If there is
a heaven "would you know my name" (Eric Clapton, 1992)
       Mary L. Procter?

Jersey Joe, Jersey Joe, Arnold Raymond Cream
       —I was four—Fletcher Walker, 1948
       Not then, then when? But remember your
fine body
       muscles rippling to get up from the canvas
       as here you flow
into the waiting arms of the referee.
like as though a tragic water, Jersey Joe Walcott
       somehow a fallen father.

This is the William Pachner Centennial: Jew
       Barely escapes Europe: 1939
Paints memories of home
       Abstract expressions of the Holocaust
       yet the defiance of jubilation
William, Happy Hundredth.

Sit down a while
among the trees and palms. Heat. Humidity.

Anoles bobbing their heads
extending red dewlaps
in Challenge and Triumph up and down
the legs of marble and bronze statues.

And back through the gallery
of Tibetan and Nepalese bronzes
Vishnu, Ganesha, remover of obstacles
(No monkeys?)   Shiva:
"I could have danced all night
I could have danced all night":
Loewe and Lerner: 1956
between your fire and your drum

and there a tiny bronze Buddha, seated
one hand beckoning,
the other pointing to the ground
the earth I'm walking on.

A Line Stolen from Rumi

Just because you woke this morning
does not require you to comment discerningly
on my blue suede shoes. I found them
by the side of a bay where weavers were spinning
foam into fibers of a brown tide on their spindles,

naked, of course, breakfasting on carrageen
and black and purple mussels. And, yes, the weather
did fine without us. And, yes, we'll not cease
to exist in these silent riffs struggling to BEcome.

Then why is my mouth filled with love words
left from last night?   Small things count. Look,
I found an alien rift opening passages
through my toast this morning. She reminds me
of the spider clinging to the fibers of her web
well passed her season or reason
to spin at all.

Being One
For Yon-Cha

So skinny were we
we both fit on a gurney
side by side
atom to atom
above below both together
being one

so skinny and
the wee child on the bench swing
swings facing the bay so small
he doesn't ask how big the gulf
the ocean beyond maybe
and we are one together

—long day behind ahead—
appointments made bills paid
the man coming to mend
the gurney   years
and more just to move in

new homes new winding
shells to build around
the soft the tender
the wounded parts
and just then
moving out again and
both skinny again   tide

at one with the moon
and the land together and the sun
and the child wee child swings
is swinging   squeak of the bench swing
going out   squeak coming in
like breathing the earth breathing
child as he swings telling stories
to his mom who joins him

on the bench swing
Atom-to-atom earth above moon below
and the sun going down
and the islands across the bay
—oceans beyond—rising
in the sinking sun sinking
under the heavy traffic
and condos, castles and
more traffic over causeways, rising
in the sun all together and we
so skinny we swing on a gurney
being one.

Dream Sequence (Flags)

The waitress approaches to take the order.
"My name is Cleopatra. Call me Patsy.
I will be yours."

Catty-cornered to where you are seated
the child is five or six, with hair marcelled
James Joseph Brown style and satiny skin
dark chocolate hue. "How beautiful his hair.
How fine. Your mom must love you very much."
"Yes, Mommy loves me very much."

Pizza arrives, medium size. The mind
fumbles backward to the moment you may
have ordered pizza. Cleopatra (Patsy)
reveals the splicing wheel and slices it
in half, then slices once again, this time
perpendicular to the first wound. Two
more cuts diagonal to the first two
make eight slices with X marking the spot.

The woman now sitting across from you
is Veronika with a *k,* adult
exchange student from Hungary. And, marveled,
you hand a slice to her, which has become
a precious thing, a lodestar jewel of sorts.
Patsy is gone. You smell rivers;
Nile and Amazon among them.

"Only in Amerika" Veronika
whispers, her voice is rich and textured;
her accent, studied, drawn out...nocturnal.
"Only in America," breaches the rim
of the dream like the mantra of an old
and grievous history.

Flag upon flag in front of each home
pierced by the headlight as you are driving
though sheets of blinding snow, as if all
the world had been forgotten and all but
the most forgotten must be reminded
of the name of home.

Veronika sits beside you though fading
like the last remaining memory of her:
"Only in Amerika." You gaze upward
toward the moon...lodestars of remorse
cry like children in the night.

A Nap a Dream a Wish

I take naps mostly but each waking
dream is the same story, settling itself
into advancing keyboards, rhythms and sliding
doors illuminating the walls. I expected

a text of intricately patterned and finely woven
wool to slip comfortably over my eyes, but not
this trace of a love song, like a face woven
into a tapestry: a second thought blooming to
the full fruition that it had always been:
you and me entangled like two quanta
or two stars in a single monologue. I know

it was mostly you, but how to pin you down
to one person seen on a street, whose shoulders
I could gently caress and whom gently,
though less gently, admonish: "Now listen
here...listen, hear..." I was trying

to say you as though that were the way
only to wish you into being , but you
were always being—typing letters, sending postcards,
watching the music advance across your backyard window
—chameleon that you are, I understand...

as we all, each of our telescopic eyes
high in its turret, focusing on
different worlds and ways of being
just us, until the prey, as we pray, happens
before us, conflates the many "I's"

our eyes have made of us into one being again:
all hungers, love and attention focused
on that which is essential for consumption
at this moment...is what I

wished to tell you, prey as we are
to each other's need and wont, as
the monologue continues about and
around us, wishing so much to be
just us, as I napped and dreamed
awake and napped again.

In Passing: Nature

Isn't that what you'd expect in the first place:
just one day after Earth Day, she picks up
all her marbles, gets on her high horse
and leaves in a huff? Meanwhile

angry smokestacks looming in the distance
puffed, stiffening their resistance
to strings, wax, nature
and the Clean Air Act. The beach
wasn't big enough for all of us,
anyway, let alone those fins bobbing
up and down offshore, man-friendly
or mines.   Thing is

no matter where you look doesn't bring
the horizon any closer or into clearer focus.
We have all been given license to choose
a philosophy to live by or lack thereof
—seagulls be damned as they damn those
who trespass against them, and in fact
we are

who never paid attention to each other's tantrums
and preached to silent choirs with zippers open
and our mouths full. And so,

I shall never forget how none of us,
not one, seemed able
to place a phone properly in its cradle
when phones had cradles and people
waiting at the other end, or
the many times, one of us, if not all,
was caught talking to him or herself,
back turned to the audience
and sitting in the corner.

Tacking

It happens; over night and all at once
your bladder issues have been forgiven
—if the problem was chronic, is this the fabled
ocean-cure: eight hundred pounds of roaring pachyderm
cast overboard? In the meantime

composers compose, singers sing
and all the world's scientists and religionists
gather to unfurl the subject of self
or lack thereof—the ups and downs, the heaves and ho's,
summed up in the evocation of a coastline
perceived dimly through the lozenge port-hole
of a derelict sloop.

Can I make one thing clear?
comes an exhausted plea from the bilge of things
morphing into other things, entwined in still
other things, which—returning to our thematic—
may be the sudden flight of self and no-self—a sense
of jest among good natured friends, or tacking
on the perfidy of the wind. To which comes

the response: This, the nature of the "beast,"
for even the bladder, innocent of all wrong doing,
is subject to dissection and inquisition
into the further causes of disease.

And yet, encapsulated therein is the meanwhile
we inhabit: children across the land and each sea
dingle are born un-nailed to a cross, and busy
at play. And we laugh,

and we jest. A sail. A sweet metastasis
fills the evening.

Portrait with Hula-Hoops
For Chiarina

They are near my sister's age
        —some older, some younger. So
they know things: careers, children, marriage
        —some happy, some ending in silence.
Other things they hardly mention anymore.

They are content today: Hula-Hoop Day.
The instructor—also near my sister's age—
has brought them here—tide coming in,
skimmers and gulls resting in the sand
        heads turned into the wind,
        sloops on the bay, anchored
        as though waiting.

They have brought their newly purchased hula-hoops.
The instructor twirls hers around her waist
—gyrates her hips. The hoop comes to life. Spins.
They are familiar with the feel of the hoops
—the motion, their bodies only half remember.

They are from that summer—maybe two—
when all the girls swirled hoops around their waists
        "all day," if only for the moment. My sister
clearly was the champ—clearly—

as she spun the red and green orbit
around her center,
        before the rifts—topography of unrelieved
mornings, the wordless middle passage—strapped
yokes of sorrows, unearned, unannounced
around her neck and shoulders.
where she most hurt,
        becoming her new horizon:

the weight of living never
shared but stored behind the eyes,
along the highways of her nerves
 —the ones that neither
            she nor I mention any more

Dennis

I'm here counting waves
—more ripples on this small, shallow bay—
nevertheless, it's what I do   —and

the lately returned black back skimmers,
their long black and orange clown beaks
deadly to small fish at dusk swimming
too close to the surface   —and

behind and cater-corner to me
on another bench a middle-aged woman
is pretending to read as one of the beach's homeless
is hitting her up for a handout   who will soon

be here so I lift a dollar bill from my wallet
to hand him quickly not to hear his story
—I want to get back to my counting.

Blood and mud crusted on both bare knees
and hands   he fell   says he hasn't eaten today
maybe yesterday either   he isn't sure.

I refocus when he mentions "tunnels"
"My unit dug tunnels into theirs"
—tunnels crossing tunnels   breaking into tunnels—
under Vietnam's jungles, rice and battle fields—
"We filled them with booby-traps, grenades,
bamboo slivers to step on, to spring out chest-high
                                        anything

they did it to us   we did it to them"   and

I think "tunnels" like parasite worms
winding their way through a human mind

and just then
the once besieged woman is coming over
with a bag of nuts to give to him   she didn't have
any change   but she has these nuts
he can't eat nuts   "My teeth"   and

someone else comes over from the direction
of the parking lot   with a six-pack of "Boost"
the protein drink   "Dennis, I got you this"   and leaves.

I watch him as he heads toward the parking lot
passes the volleyball courts where
a group of women have divided into teams
and are playing volleyball. They've planted
the Rainbow Flag at the side of the courts.

A mixed flock of skimmers and seagulls suddenly
fly by in front of us.   A child races behind
as if he's about to take off himself.

Once more I am focused:
"You know him?"
"Maybe"
"But he knows you...."
"I guess   I don't know
I must'of fell. I'm diabetic
I don't drink or do drugs   Been so weak
No food either   This will do me good"

Two more years in Korea guarding
Vietnamese prisoners in a POW camp   eight more
in an Indiana State Prison: Manslaughter
Mitigating circumstances
                    Posttraumatic stress syndrome

Then the story stops   "I gotta go"
Dennis gets up, fetches a volley ball
—volleyball courts just behind us—
tosses it

35

"Thanks" from a woman coming
to get the ball   A league of middle-aged women playing

He's up
He's leaving   I hand him the dollar
he gives me a poem

A Quote from the Works of John Ashbery

...On all roads
we merely trespass, finding a level
store-bought thing...

But there was more to it than that,
or why the waves rocking the derelict sloops
in the harbor? Who goes there anyway?
And who cares

if not the health inspectors concerned with the affairs of water?
All we wanted was a little candy to sweeten the breath
and to be young forever. The sea-cure won't work;
too many gulls, herring or otherwise, pecking at the porridge,
migrating, exhorting us to follow as long
as we feed them and wish them
wishful things.

But to return to my original question:
the invisible sea-monster under the bay, causing
the uncalled-for wake...time insists
this has always been the eight hundred pound
gorilla locked in the closet. And experience proves
it is wise to embrace it all and make it ours.

But, of course, I'm only pulling your hair
or pinching your cheek, or never said it
in the first place. You are a fellow traveler,
a few well-timed bobs of the head, a rustle
of wing and tail feathers can make us
all ours again.

Otherwise the page runs out with the tide.
A decent exchange of cellphone numbers and
we can meet at the corner. That murder
of crows, the percentage of parakeets will surely
have something to say about that,
can decide all that.

The Sumptuous Hills of Gulfport

For some times there was nothing to signify about;
permission had filtered down from nowhere
in particular for the dead to proceed
in burying the dead, while life went about
its business of being, each kernel bursting
at its seams—nothing wishing at the moment
to be some thing else.

By the shore, children continued to fill
their painted carousel pails with shovels-full
of water and sand, dinghies had come
to rest along side the homeless sloops
and ketches—would be sailors were content
to drink demitasse cups of memory
or watch the wings of an osprey dip
as she turned smoothly into the wind.

The writing slowed down by degrees,
came almost to a halt as process
drifted in and out of the scaffolding
of syntax and the rift continued
between the organic and the inorganic.

Like pearls
each piece of recollection "could" be strung
to another forming a story with its quanta
of "truths" revealed within the surrounding
veils of mist, if only there were a "could,"
if only a "will" as verbs grew less transitive
and subjects drifted like sail boats farther
and farther away from the cooling objects
of their desire.

The shoreline—pails and all—was slowly drifting
into being. There were the "I's," the "you's,"

"he's," "she's," "we's," and "they's" also
drifting into process, indifferent, maternal

depending on the time of day, or of waking,
or falling back to sleep.

Tampa Bay I

If you accept the possibility
of a parenthetic afternoon and

a ray or two of setting sun escaping
from spaces remaining between condos, and

the pelican preening out on the bay
the temporary good nature of gulls,

and one young girl who teaches cartwheels to
another, younger still, perhaps her sister

then we are all King Midas and each thing,
touched by our longing, is gold

Tampa Bay II

How can I end this poem which
I have yet to begin? We—the plurals of we—
were just sitting there, in a kind of parenthesis or bubble
—like random though not unhappy bits of flotsam—
that occurs just for minutes after sunset
when the bay's agitation
                                    settles down
to mirror smoothness, sucked clean of solar energy
                                                            or
(as I like to think)
                        simply to rest from bearing the weight
of earth's daily commerce
                                or none of the above
as is so much we touch with our longing a product
of "none of the above"—mere collision of real
and virtual particles, which have somehow disappeared
        into a dimension we have no certain knowledge of.

                        Just sitting there
—as I am—in mirror smoothness, though rattled still
by this project lacking a beginning...is it that

real living, pure living (pura vida
as they say in little Costa Rica, penciled in
between its Atlantic and Pacific beaches) may
only take place at these moments—the sudden stoppage
of traffic on a busy freeway when we were only out
                                    for a random ride

Or the moment of the unexpected gaze at a cliff
where a thousands-year-old hand print on a rock surface
proclaims "I was here"—someone was here, but who?

or
a kiss on the cheek (that for no reason

should be different from any other kiss) suddenly drains
the soul of all its "busy commerce"
and is baptismal in a time before baptism

                                     —the pure life
stuck like a vein of gold at the bottom
of a mine otherwise dug from greed?

In other words:
                        where to end when I don't know
where it begins, cannot step beyond
the margins of the poem to view it
as a distant wholeness
                                    where words
begun in the simple sound of breath,
the pumping of the singular heart   end
not far away.

Speculation.
Or diagnosis based on solid Physics
of a flat universe
                        extending to where the eternal
may no longer reach
                            Islands adrift beyond their very light and echo.

Heady just to imagine
when there is so little to go on:
a half remembered fable from a golden book,

a singular gaze
—your gaze who may be hearing or reading this

or thinking this
                        as if once upon a time
we were all mirrors of each other, with the same "spin
on things," the universe, say,repeating in compassion what each
reflection said
in a field of ripples, we ourselves created
as it went about creating us
—this parenthetic moment when

a sloop drifting at half sail requests
our undivided though momentary attention
and an osprey
                    wheels round in midair
dips then turns away deciding the object
of its desire has descended to depths
                                     beyond its ken.

It strikes me as if all this wonder that is you
or we—the many plurals of we—for that matter, and
all that surrounds us were contained in this one

parenthesis—bubble of sorts that suddenly inflates
as if from nowhere, between the nothing of before
                          and that which follows

or
           maybe it is only the sun's afterglow
calms the waters running deep within
as the true light sinks behind those condos
on the outer bank, where meals
are now being prepared, TVs turned on
a meme is being posted to FB:

"This is a test. Only one person out of ten
will copy and paste this to their wall,
if only for the next ten minutes
or the continuing eons
                    whichever come first."

"Tender Mercies": Poem Adaptation

These are hard to understand;
bear with me, laugh with me...
or at. See what thread in the frieze
recurs at the corner of your eye. Stay.

In the outer patios where only children
were allowed to play, old men whirl
in circles, like old dreams
gathered in a mirror. She sees,

obeys a season within—climbs
into her SUV in pursuit of sunset:
a story ending in rubble
—the blue seep between the rocks,
"a certain moment of respite"

Still there? The silence at the end
of the phone spoke towering
antennas of pure space
—pure being. Hold me

at the corner of your glance.
Dawn brings a distant rumble
of mountains, the drum roll
within.

Child in the Lake

> the wreck and not the story of the wreck
> the thing itself and not the myth:
> — Adrienne Rich

Maybe the surprise of the attack
suppressed the pain to follow. Those bitten
by a shark during a summer swim
in calm gulf waters often claim so.
We shall never know.

The media are not enough:
coverage of the divers, explanations
of the search and rescue gear.
the tiny wrapped package delivered
to the open back doors
of the waiting ambulance. The obligatory
interview with the neighbor who
has known them for years.   Not enough.

But as if we must probe the ancient lineage
of the attacker, whose essence is not to kill
but to hunger; trace the length and weight
of its skill as it stalks, estimates
the size of this or that package of nourishment
—and the silence of its approach, like
water flowing through water—evolution
of random energies turned to focused matter
and will,

must pronounce the exact words
concerning the father's hands
succumbing to the greater power
of relentless jaws—the plunge
to the mud bottom of the lake.

And the child in the lake
whose whole life has been till now only presence;

what past terror to compare it to
or is it only surprise he feels?
We must configure the divers
not as divers, but as those who
first glimpse the white form
almost aglow among the algae
and mud at the bottom of the lake

who know that alligators
have no teeth to chew and tear
but only sharpened white pegs
to hold and drag their catch
to a safe place and wait
as acid waters hasten the journey
of flesh to softened matter.

And the two figures seated
in the front seats of the auto
on their journey back to their safe northern home,
empty child seat that follows,
empty seat at the family table
no sense of closure
—doors that never close

no sense of rubbing it from memory
to make it less virulent, less real
no sense but for the words
that moor us to the edge of entropy:
a voice to stir the silence
reconfigure the abyss
and not the myth.

The Zumba Class

For Ellen Noto, poet

Because you come to the dance
like a tentative spirit in a grown woman's body
as if once again acquainting yourself
with a rhythm that had always been welled up
deep in your body
                        which is a kind of soul

and because
                        you come to most things
—great and small as we say—similarly
touching, feeling
                        as on those nights
with their stars
the dimmest of which may only reveal themselves
from the corner of our eyes

and to stare directly at them
were as if to cause a blush
in a physical system not made to blush
and they are gone

or like
that moment on that wooden platform path
through what remains of the Old Florida
—the oldest Florida—before the invasion
of the white fever, before even the shell
collectors and hammock raisers

the Florid Land before good and evil
with only cycles like tides exchanging
death for life and life for death
in manatee estuaries of time—no one
        to name the simple intricacy
        of the pattern, the dance

47

and on the pathway between cross-planks
        so carefully positioned and nailed down
that between them nearly nothing could fit
you spotted the dead anole lizard
        whose corpse between the planks
indeed did fit

and the moment
we decide not to move it
to a "safer" place
                and leave
the limp creature there where chance
has found the resting place and
will make of it what can be made

like
the discovery of a rhythm in a dance
the path of the weave
                and more
as each wave reaching a shoreline is more.

Message from the Board of Trustees
For John and Rudy, Nell and Karen

for all gays and lesbians,
bisexual and transgendered persons

and all the undecided and unsure
and for all the little boys tucked away in attics
who gaze at themselves
in dusty mirrors, more comfortable
in Mom's or sis's clothes, and all the little girls
who gaze at themselves
in dresses feeling that their being
has been replaced in a mistaken body
as if through some implacable magic,

you may come out now. New theories are
in the works, coming down the chutes:
It wasn't your mothers' fault for loving
or possessing too much,
or your father's fault, however much
he was absent or simply didn't care;

and least of all, your fault for the crush
you had in grammar school on your teacher
who was a woman and you were a girl
or was a man and you were a boy.

New theories indicate that
—a myriad of conflations of genes...
conditions in the uterus during
fetal development.... Studies among
primitive hunter/gatherer tribes
providing further evidence...
gender selection and identification
on a sliding scale—
you may come out now.

And for all of you,
who, like faggots, heated the flames
so that God's more grievous offenders
could be more easily burned at the stake,
and all of you who never cried because
"Big girls don't cry"...it was all a mistake;

and for all of you who perished
anonymously in anonymous hospital beds
where no one came to wipe the sweat from your heads
or clean a wound or merely scratch
the tip of your nose,
which you could not longer reach,

your relatives have been informed
—albeit through the liberal media.
Your moms and dads now know:
They can bury your ashes.
All is forgiven...all forgotten.

And to all
the young men longing between love and lust
and loneliness who have been lured by other young men
into an alley or deserted field
where other young men eagerly waited
to steal their money, beat and maybe kill them

and to all the young women who were shown
what a real man feels like and,
in the process of learning,
were beaten and maybe killed

because in both cases you "deserved" what was coming to you,
because you were queer
or a dike....all has been made right. Only
for your sake, be less provocative,
for some of our young friends
are still given, if not addicted, to "wilding."

And you, James Schuyler,
Frank O'Hara, Elizabeth Bishop,
write your sweetest love poems.
It was all a mistake.
All is forgiven.

The Water Poem

I was happy then. And tonight
—past dinner and talk of that one time,
the good time—herds of water buffalo
roll in the calm clean mud at the bank of

a river as gazelles in flight press
themselves against the moon. Brief,
you confessed, these sudden pools at the end
of a wood that approach us as if in a dream;
hardly pools but chambers of dark water
where they float—emerald, ruby—glowing
in a moment of light. But what are they...
old, reptilian, unchanging? And for this

nothing need take place—a good thing
merely to browse on the new grass
rising from the shallow bay bottom, to roll
on a wave, mermaid-like, open your eyes
better to dream the sun,
able to put down the bones we have harvested
and gnawed on and picked on.

You see then how the deepening loss and
even gain have brought us here, how a single
tern may pitch and dive above us
as we breach and dive—massive, collective
foldings and unfoldings returning to
a sea in love with her children.

Glass Ceiling

Nothing in the evolution of insect
DNA predicts the presence of glass.

The August yellow jacket, deprived
by the queen, her mother's hormones,
of progeny, now battles with glass.

She has abandoned the morsel of meat whose scent
led her through the closing door of the low-carb-
cal restaurant and now beats herself against the glass.

Energy depleted, she will drop to the sill by our seats,
walk crazily about; until recovered, she resumes
her flight into the glass.

Each confrontation with glass
is a first confrontation with glass.

She does not forget the glass is there;
she cannot record glass is there.

Her areal passage around trees, bushes,
stems of flowers, flowers, leading to her underground
home of paper, are there, duly recorded

—map to the hexagonal chambers
where hungry larvae, not hers, wait
like squirming pieces of an impossible, living gnocchi.

For all this information evolution has left
receptacles along the double helix of
her DNA, but not for glass.

Glass has no definition
—solid liquid, crystal without form:

impossible product of fire.
Yellow jackets are the evolution
of another fire, organic, liquid fire
drips from her workers barren ovipositor.

The glass means nothing to her. There are no
metaphors. Only glass.

Concerning the Carapace of a Box Turtle

Seen from the inside of the great dome
along the high arch, the backbone emerges
as though from a sea
of white porous rock

—the unfinished sculpture, half out
like a half-fulfilled dream or project
of anguish and strength, each

vertebra distinct, as are the two ribs
sprouting from each one, only to sink
back shortly into the white solid sea:

design of no previous plan but wrought
from the hazards of epochs
—lodged in the gamble of a given moment—

yet nothing emerges, really, or sinks
back into the calcium base, but rather
each vertebra, each rib constructs

around itself the mantle
that is now the solid white dome
—each rib, as it were, beginning like a premonition
of what one day would become a flying buttress
(though internalized), a secret not to be imagined
nor even realized until an eternity after
by the hand of another species;

the skeleton itself breaching muscle
and skin to shield the body
and, in turn, itself in the flattened
substance that is also our nails,
or the scale covering of fish,
the fur of a common mammal,

the feather of a bird,
mottled a dull orange or deep yellow
with rivers of dark amber, so that
it now fits among a matting of forest leaves,
briefly lit in the rays of the passing autumn sun

Exiting the Cathedral Church of St. John: The Great Divine

Somewhere at the juncture
of Revival Gothic and Romanesque arches
the work of mason in stone ceases

Structure opens to the harmonic whim
of the organic   grows upward exceeding
limit   returns exhaling and once again
expands   As we diminish, return

to our elements: longing   fulfillment
fire   water   Descending toward us
the once plaster and marble saints melt
they themselves returning to the elemental:

mythos of flesh changed to spirit
spirit to flesh   Sounds echo
among the chasm of wall, pillar and arch
words become the longing of wolves
the love songs of whales

All world stirs to life and us
reduced to our simple holy matter   Things
that were not ours—brick   stone   the wild dream
of construction—now are us   as times later we

exit the great Bronze West Doors   breach the surface
of the street dressed in a new kind of cloth
born to our own beating hearts
new light flooding the mind

Concerning Elephants

The night vision of elephants is only slightly more acute
than our own at perceiving the profiles
of the blue lionesses stalking in the bush, but does little
to make their proximity less dangerous,

hence the reluctance of their footsteps,
the mortal stillness at the end of their senses.
On the other hand,

they have no hands, relying on their trunks
for smell and touch, which explains
the gentle swaying of heads when they caress
the bones of ancestors and other lost loved-ones,
reminded again of their souls that once
held together these broken scaffolds
of bones;

for despite the magnitude of size and time,
they seem to make no distinction between
what once was flesh and what once was soul.

As for the feet of elephants, they stand deprived of all forms
of writing, and can be used only on their endless treks
between dry plains and water—sand and fodder—
and to hear the earth as she whispers
a sense of place at registers
only elephants may hear.

On a scale of one to ten, elephants
range mostly in the feminine
with the time-outs a matriarch may take
so that offspring of the clan may be
amazed at the mysteries of their trunks,

or that she herself may stand bemused by
or in fearful awe of the rage of a bull

whose musth time is often dangerous
though not without its delicious charm.
The principal trend among elephants
is neither belief nor disbelief. Like most nomads,
they are shadowed by a sense of loss

in a seemingly endless rosary of homes
interrupted on occasion when one old matron
—or even an old bull, alone on the veldt—
remembers the taste of lush plain
in flower, or the feel of a distant cousin
or sister or brother,
or the blood of the blood of the blood of
a loved one, latent in their bones.

Recollection of Lydia Longstreth Hunt
in memoriam

She rises from the goo of daydreams
like a three dimensional copy, but real.
Who are you? And she who has been dead
these many years is seated on the steps
of the 42nd Street Library. It is

lunchtime, you eat like a bird...seeds,
bits of fresh and dried fruit, slivers of almond,
you shall live a long time, but hasn't as
the obit from the West Coast university
where she shone now points out to her honor

which you read online, like a bit of parchment
now faded—though pink shine in cyberspace and she, of course
understands this, your concern, of course...for once
before it happened: lines of communication
broken down...of understanding, broken branch

in flood time...floated away, though who are we
to suppose how lives go on living like a debt left
unpaid, if ever even owed: happy life though *breve*,
"*el sueño es breve*," the dream short though happy,
her short, happy life, now

at her second home: a lovely street in Buenos
Aires...the fresh good air...and nearby: La Recoleta
recollection: Domingo Faustino Sarmiento, his nemesis,
Facundo Quiroga (your dissertation on Lugones), all
buried here, the common ground: statesman, caudillo,

modernist writer as they struggle for nation,
but the struggle—understood, misunderstood—all
water under your bridge and the bridge, like a branch,
floating away to the sea atop the Silver River
unperturbed, maternal..."I wanted to be

with these remnants of my family..." but not today,
today young office workers, mermaids and men flow
from office buildings, remembered now from
my bench in a small town placed at the edge
of the mild Gulf Coast, as other benches

and tables settle down to flank the steps
of the library and take their places in the gardens
behind the building where the city has commissioned
a band to play...today—a day like a poem reluctant to end—
lunches spread themselves across the tables...food vendors,

Ph.D. candidates, like us, leak slowly drop by drop from
the main entrance, like bats, blinking at the sun,
settle down on the steps flanked by the two lions to eat
lunches tasting of theories of semiotics—we've
deconstructed ourselves all morning—

and forgetting or not even knowing,
as you didn't know, that she has been dead
for years, has lived encapsulated in a Google obit,
you ask her if theory may also be a food
for the obsessed, like us, obsessed, as if

old mimes, writers and actors had got it right, or,
at least partially, for in fact,
de hecho, la vida may very well be *sueño*
or dream within many dreams...the very core
of this good breeze flowing north along 5th Avenue

to meet another from the East along 42nd Street
encircling us in this atmospheric charm
—candidates and workers alike: the what, the how,
the wear and tear and why, I ask her,
but she doesn't answer, she is gone.

Portrait of a Woman in her Garden

Nuestras vidas son los ríos
que van a dar en la mar,...
— Jorge Manrique

We've been this way before—the city
slackening, relaxing into suburbs,
once small towns themselves, a farm, the graveyards,
a church on a low rising hill—like travelers
on a train as the landscapes pass us by
—a beach town, the unfailing sea beyond.

Therefore, it is incumbent upon us
to consider the woman in her garden...
to step carefully through these fields
—the lush labyrinth of life from its beginnings
to these ends, incumbent upon us

to consider her labor. It is mid-July,
—mid-summer—as she bends to run
her fingers along the leaves and stems
of the tomato vines for aphids. She recalls
there are species of ants that keep aphids
as we keep cows. They carry the insects
to the plants on which they feed
—tomatoes for instance. As they suck
the juices from the plants, the ants "milk" them,
stroking their sides with their antennae
to release the sweet substance the aphids
excrete and the ants are unable to resist,
as one day we perhaps could not resist
a glass of cold milk... "Lady Bug,

Lady Bug, fly away." Ladybugs
and their nymphs are avid consumers of aphids.
She likes the sound of that; the alliteration
and assonant rhyme. She goes

to the corn, beans and winter squash next.
Once on a small farm—a chacra—
in the Northern Andes, she saw these three plants
growing from a single mound. Seneca women
thousands of miles in time, where she stands now,
planted this very way—each plant according
to its nature contributing to the growth
of the others: the Three Sisters... Marigolds,
aromatic herbs border the garden.
Their scent repels hungry insects. Nevertheless

the reds and yellows, mixing with oranges
among the green herbs are quite lovely.
...as though beauty were its own reason.
Why? Where does it come from, she wonders?

She picks a weed here, leaves another to its
own small life... From dreams? But where
do the dreams come from? She's read that at times
a chimp, transfixed, may stare for minutes
—for hours?— at a waterfall as if in wonder.
Does beauty therefore proceed from wonder?
...The stillness of beauty in change. The way
a waterspout produces the same arc, though
the millions of gallons of water, shot through,
is nothing if not change. The way

a garden changes from year to year
—crop rotations, the arbitrary rains,
the sudden frosts of early spring...
what we may control and what we cannot.

She considers all this: an abstract painting
framed in flowers and herbs, but living,
mutating from year to year, or within
a single season, a single hour.

In three months the garden will be nothing.
The first frost of October silences the rasp
of katydids, the strumming of the crickets.
The woman passes through her kitchen,
from the window of which she glances
at the garden, to her workroom where she reads,
writes, sketches. How do you preserve
a garden? Can you paint it in words?

Beyond the garden are woodlands, planted fields,
churches, graveyards and small towns
flowing, so to speak, into larger cities,
becoming suburbs with no memory
of the towns they were: larger and larger
populations with more intricate crossings,
connections, passions, wants, needs
similar to those of the garden, but within
all of which, the garden—so small—disappears.

Yet a memory, or perhaps, a concept remains,
this one field within larger and more complex fields
—a life within a history of lives that came before
(and after?) All within one history.
Therefore it is incumbent upon us
to consider the woman, herself,
here, as the garden, itself, is here, waiting,
and the beach beyond.

Tide

For John Migiiaccio, in memoriam

This poem comes by easily
like that time after a storm
when the ocean takes back its great breath
and the tide comes   and goes

—faithful—bringing and taking.
Inland we hear of great devastation
—rumored, only vaguely—losses
no one can or may account for. Here

parts of the island have gone missing—posts
from rotting piers where cormorants sat,
wings stretched out to the sun. Many have perished.
Some have survived, we among them.

The poem makes you think of long pieces of silk
you run through your fingers, the feel of child hair
or of night long ago when the air turned
to lavender and the presence of dark satin.

Easily the poem takes you there, word
after word, like leaves that—colorful—abandon
their trees in autumn...an old man who sits
in his backyard by the small fire he's lit.

But he's not old. Dinner was hours ago.
You sit beside him. You don't know when,
though in the course of summer, crickets have
replaced the fire flies—we called them lightning bugs:

light making way for sound, the way memory
gives way to words and words come back
to memory. You both sit by the fire.
Night goes on without you, yet you are there.

The old man is old again. People—friends,
his daughters—help him to his chair. His wife
watches, waits. He opens his vest to the sun.
No need for the fire. The fire is out.

You have gone to the tip of the island.
Vineyards have replaced potato fields; breezes
from the sea temper the hot rays of the sun
as the grapes ripen. You taste fine red wines,

bring back a bottle. There was always wine
by the fire. Tide follows tide. The old man
is left aglow by the fire. Easily memory slips
into memory. Easily the poem goes by.

Inauguration

After James Schuler or Frank O'Hara
IN MEMORIAM
For Carmella, Loretta and Marianne

Morning fresh and river fresh   what
am I doing here so early   first of the cicadas
replacing the last of the crickets. Yesterday

I thought I saw you in the Adirondack chair
that used to sit by the gate opening to the garden
but it was a shadow or a light, or light
and shadow. And the garden. Little Jake

was driving cousin little Jack in Jake's
new electric kiddy-mobile neither paying
much attention to going forward or backward
more focused on how the wheels were turning
everything is turning

And so many flowers

I only recognize the rose-of-Sharon bushes
the first buds of mums, the patches of Phlox?
Vetch? I get them mixed up and me making
my third trip to the florist: one
for myself, one for the three daughters,
one for my sister

and for once I am writing with purpose.

So many flowers
—mostly roses or carnations. The newly arrived
and newly wed couple brought trays of lasagna
—not our usual recipe but so good all the same
Everyone brings something. Those five-foot
long hero sandwiches—two. Plates
of macaroni and potato salads...pastries
"Who's gonna eat all that food?" Yet

it all goes. It all goes.
And the daughters   in the kitchen
in the patio   on the lawn   making
sure everyone gets something to eat
to drink. Everyone doing something.
Their mother cries, laughs, remembers, forgets.
Anger, love, accusation, forgiveness
battle like currents from opposing seas.

For the little ones it's all a party all a game:
Christmas mixed with birthdays. Landon
at the hoops from Texas all the way here.
Jake and Jack just as happy to go back
as forth, around in circles right there on the lawn

in front of the swimming pool
where the garden used to be.

Homage for H. Palmer Hall

I

Time then was not clicked from an overstuffed
cushion in a heated salon. Winter was an empty bin
of oats or rye, the barren udders
of an old cow. By April strong urges
shot through plant roots. Trees in first bloom
"whispered of old endings and new beginnings."
Thoughts turned to Thomas à Becket and Bath.

On the continent...the shrine of Santiago
de Compostela. By the time pilgrims
crossed the alpine springs and flowers
of the Pyrenees, they'd forgotten
the muddy streets of Paris, the squalor of Rome.

But Jerusalem was always the prize;
city of old rancors, remnants of walls,
ashes of burnt offerings—crusaders, jihadists...
all young and hoping "to do something,
to travel, to see what was or life would be like"...
streets smelling of roasting lamb parts,
of human and camel offal. But always
the promise down one more winding street:
a piece of Veronica's veil, a splinter
from the true cross, a glint of the Holy Grail.

Pilgrims, rich enough, packed up mules, servants,
slaves...one year out, one year back. If he were
richer, he could hire someone to make the journey
for him. They had only to bring back a palm
to prove they'd gone. These were the palmers,
this, an age of faith. And from them, you
derive your name, the long name

that utters its first syllable when cold hands
deliver you to the light, grows as you grow:
the face you see in the mirror. The mirror
doesn't lie.

II

As a child you were a palmer of sorts
in the back seat of a succession of cars
as you recall it—as were we all—between
Beaumont, Texas and Wakulla Bay, Florida:
the southeastern arch of the country: land

meeting sea in an embrace of marshes,
bogs, mangrove belts where geography meets
and mates with itself bringing more of itself
to the light, "*a la luz*" as they say
farther south.

What seeps into a new mind sprung between
land and sea—oaks mourning down
in Spanish moss, and scattered among the green,
cabbage palms and palmettos...is yours.

Low tide and the stench of rotten eggs,
life beginning and ending. Mosquitoes
light on new skin, buzz through your sleep
like the subtext of a dream. Something molds
a path into you, growing ever inward
as you grow outward to meet your world.

—Wood storks: the sleek body of an ibis
and the naked head of their raptor ancestors;
anoles, flashing their red dewlaps like
flags proclaiming this leaf is mine,
this strip of bark, mine...at night
a gecko glows green under lamplight,
takes a moth and is gone...flights

70

of pelicans more pterosaur than bird.
El lagarto, "alligator" (named by Spanish
conquistadores waking, perhaps,
from a bad dream that brings no gold
but early death), basks on a river bank
in a patch of sun, absorbing through
the third lids of its eyes the pure
intensity of life.

A pilgrimage continued over long summers,
circuitous, penetrant, saturated
by smaller journeys, daily,
to the mail box, two miles away from
the house of your grandmother
down an oak lined road (where once
you cut your foot kicking a can
and remember the scar years later
as shrapnel pierces your other foot
on an sudden and unlikely battle field
in Viet Nam), adrift
in small row boat
with only the luck of tides to bring you home.

Your only choice is to live.
Later the memories—joy, regret—
another matter, living and dying another life:
a poem pressed into a leaf torn free
in autumn.

III

As you grow there were other journeys, trips
to nowhere, mad runs in a new Mustang:
Texas to Florida and back; follow
the Mississippi to Saint Louis, east
then to New York...you, a friend, and two young

71

women of your age and need for movement, whom
you've met along the way. One night, all four,
half drunk and all alive...a moon, maybe, above the bay
in Gulfport, Louisiana, a sunrise over Beaumont,
sunset over Wakulla.

What is the palm you, or any of us, bring back
if only to yourself? The time between
the protean and some call
to duty? Wild run up the coast,
quick stop to watch the night,
one more kiss, deep, passion
for these particular moments
within a wider, deeper passion
—each second adds another syllable to the name.

IV

Then there was a war. Not a great war, as you say.
Mostly it was the poor who went,
a small portion of the committed, another
larger one of undecided, as you were.
And the escapes to Canada, flights to Europe.

All in all, not that many deaths
(if we don't count the Vietnamese
as we never do). Names carved on a black stone
wall to remind us (though mostly we forget).
A drop in the bucket, really...

next to the Great War and the greater war
that followed... By certain standards
not much greater than Antietam or the final count
of the dead on the fields of Gettysburg...
An even smaller drop:

—perhaps, no drop at all, really: One night,
another distant land where I too am called
to serve, a young man, younger than I, is
holding a small knife to my stomach, reason
as unimportant now as it was absurd then.

Like a lacuna within a greater narrative
of fear is my fixation on the minute size
of the instrument of death in proportion
to its magnitude: much like
the parenthesis that is life.

In a language as new to me as the land,
I argue like a lawyer. I win the case.
I'm not sure. Maybe it's a kilometer
to my hotel. I don't know exactly
the length of a kilometer.

Nor the duration of fear. It grows
as I turn the key and enter my room,
hatches the next morning and the next
like a bird of prey as I shower. I take
this fear to be text and subtext of war...

yet only a part, even in the small war
you played your part in
as a "bat linh"—captured soldier—
Vietnamese for an enlisted man, the language
the army has taught you to learn.

The other drops I don't know: the waiting,
the count and boredom of days before
a sudden burst of motors, the crack
of rifle from a tree: life at the edge of life...
the child who stares blankly at you

from the back of a buffalo calmly chewing
its cud. Her stare leaves a stain

at the back of your mind, and it hangs there
in your poems like a chrysalis waiting to
hatch from under a leaf on a tree.

One day, translating radio transmissions,
you killed a man—those are your words.
You pick up the "enemy" voice, calling
positions to his forces. He identifies
himself, "I am Bao."

And through triangulations, "Napalm
and shit happens." A name in life.
And you without seeing,
add one more name
to the names of death.

Years pass. Life goes on unabated
inhabiting new bodies, leaving old ones behind.
One day in a car dealership, the one whose eyes
you meet is a fellow soldier. The text and subtext
are still there. The stain is still there.

It hunkers down, itself like a soldier
wanting to live or die at the same time. The wars,
like life, move on...Gaza to the Sudan...
A Yazide child crying through the night...
What choice is there?

V

The journey, as always, ends where it's begun:
A woman, an unlikely woman...an English orphan
shipped on a square-rigger to America: stepdaughter or chattel.

She is the Jerusalem of your summers from Beaumont,
to Wakulla Bay. From her you learn the odor of wood-framed porches,
the tide coming and going across a tidal flat, the click of fiddler crabs

on guard at their tunnel entrances, waving their one giant
claw like a challenge to the sun. This becomes the new norm
for a growing boy: conflation of senses to wake you

from a sticky afternoon in a Beaumont, Texas
grammar school or a walk on a mud road
with rice fields and mines in Viet Nam.

As much ancestor as grandmother. Married at fifteen
to a much older Confederate warrior, more wedded
to the war of Northern Aggression than to her,

she gives children to the light of Florida, nurses
their fevers, mourns the death of one, befriends
black fisherman, out on the bay at night,

their lanterns resting in the bows of their rowboats
shine like low stars through a velvet night. A random
laugh drifts in from the bay...a fish is caught. From

England to the front porch of an aged woman,
chattel to mother. Orphan to fisher woman.
She had her visions, did what she could.

Palmer,
you end your journey wondering was it enough,
what chances you missed taking out of fear,
what straw to grasp among the straws to grasp.

The palm a child takes home on Palm Sunday
is a straw also. A lily is a straw... All grasses.
So it must be a straw you bring back:
the name of things, yours...ours...
the long name, name of time,
the unpronounceable name.

Autumn Leaf Fest

What had to happen, happened, though
no one noticed. You were all distant stars
and there I was, a sixty-year-old, out
at midnight on Broadway, playing to angels
in my underwear.

What clothes would fit the supple cloth
we had woven? Had the water in our cups
already run over? And all the while,
like a voice born deep within a white wall,
it was saying: "These days I write like crazy.
I pick the finest spring and fall white birch
though my message is always the same, though

around its edges where it curves into those
deeper valleys of knowledge and regret, things
do recall themselves, like the next breath
of a jazz improv or Baroque fugue. Where
are the notes running from and who
are they running to?" Will you buy all this?

...as though we had all become hawkers
in a countless, traveling, roadside flea market
wondering what novelties are left to sell.
I never pretended to more; these blue hills
(or is it grass?) go on with or without us
and hardly notice. I only wanted this spot.

And you have come for the parade.
Old and new plates and plastic silverware
dangle like unheard voices from the tree
branches. Your place is on the blanket. Here.
Sit down. Help yourself.

About a Woman and her Son

A slew of rusted words, snatches of phrases,
random images—half dreamt, half real—will
evoke a rhythm, a kind of cradle to rest in.

The rhythm will be about a woman and her son
—she, 27...28; he, eight or nine as she
parks the SUV and they slide
from their seats onto the asphalt
of their parking space

and gather their paraphernalia
—blue folding chair, striped blankets and towels,
bottled water—they will need
for the afternoon at this Gulf beach.

She will be blond, as well as her son,
slightly thick around the waist, and arms
—more a sign of strength, purpose in movement
than the leisure of long coffee mornings.

Young. Blond.

And now
they are passing over the dunes, careful
to use the designated walkways,
for the dunes are fragile, fragile the sea grapes,
prickly pear cacti, and the grasses growing there
a cricket rasping tentatively,
a tiny black snake slipping by, fragile
this truce between the houses on one side
and the sea.

They have reached the shore, put down
blankets, towels...unfolded chairs.
The boy has made for the wavelets
breaking nearby. The weather has been calm.

She looks to him then west
out into the Gulf. But the Gulf goes on.
It doesn't end at Corpus Christi
where shrimp boats manned by Vietnamese
refugees are putting into harbor
with their nightly catch,

nor farther down the coast to Yucatán
where tourists skim flat stones
over turquoise waters and Mayan inscriptions
have lain unread for hundreds of years.

The Gulf is endless.

The woman is endless.
And her son.

Mere Tension in the Air

I like the sound of it all
the feel at night as it brushes
across my face—tentative
as the line between two colors
a minor chord as one continues down
a country road....the same but now changed—

while filaments of its being weave themselves
into those regions where, as children, they warned us
never to go   But it is here now: tapestry
of gold thread leading to this not unpleasant
nowhere of being: the ring at the end
of the carousel ride

The familiar newness of it all hovers
just above the surface and at the edge
of it all...for all this time we have been dealing
with just such fragile stuff...surely...
without knowing   A sleight of hand
and it disappears   Poof! See? It's gone!

Yet never for too long...like a tune
played on the fragment of a flute eked out
from the bone of a tiny antelope, now extinct...gone:
mastodons floating away in caravans
on a breath   And we also

have a part to play, pithy or not;
wherefore the prelude in the pit has ended
its chords echoing as the curtain rises
Go out there! Break a leg! We cannot help
but be drawn to the feel of it all

It's the Wonder

...how easy...as if part
of our double-helix... From the eye
slides easily into our chest of memorabilia
where the patinas of rare metals are stored
—the sound of a falcon's dive
to its prey, the color

or the sudden chaos of green parrots, come to life
—aliens from an illegal land, here in the land
of the Carolina parakeet, now gone. Not the word
but the sound of green. "All sonnets say

the same thing. What does it matter what
they say?"—Williams. The sound.
And we know when we see it and then
it's gone. "We merely trespass"—Ashbery—

yet the trespass is nutritious, sustaining,
as the hunter's kill quartered on the butcher's table.

The price of living is loss:
"*Orfandad de ofandades*," César Vallejo wrote
"Orphanhood of orphanhoods," yet
he would not give up on living.

And we know the saga of the pearl,
the bathos of the onion. The sudden touch
of skin to skin, hand on hand.
The sound, the color.

Reading *April Galleons*

> And where do the scraps of meaning come from?
> — John Ashbery

I am reading Sargasso again: all
I had missed: rags of alga, half submerged, half
easing into the sun, lone
ecosystems each
no one shall know about or care about, carrying

away dots of hatchling loggerheads and
elvers; genetic maps like traceries
locked into their heads as one day they
lumber onto a beach out of this memory
to place their eggs, or hunt through
the muck at the mouth of a small river
cleansing the land as it slowly washes
it away—a dream

in their minds which their minds may never know
of seas once again, the Sargasso grass. Then,

I suppose it has always been about children:
Alexis and McKenzie who sit in the photo
near the edge of my desk as though
at the edge of a night-world
washed in a tide that is always time;
little Nicholas and tiny Sudarshan
—they may never meet—and me, in the middle

so old my bones are no more than cartilage
rebirthing in this opposite of womb.
Who, I ask opening the book, are you
locked in that motion picture that
hasn't reached an end, and when you do,

will go on without you, without so much
as a wave goodbye? Curious,

on one of the Esmeralda Islands
you may now see a gesture
meaning "to approach"
to the average assembled tourist
resembles a wave goodbye.

Then, shall we always be here to pick up
opposing signals, becoming toys
of our own games? There were beaches
there too, our theater: Saturdays,
Sargasso of games laid out
on the kitchen table. How far,

really, do we live from a kind of shore:
bluff looking over an ocean,
beach covered in clam and oyster shells,
fronting a sheltered bay with its ferries
and places to go, or a tiny river
at its mouth, flowing into a small port
with rusty trawlers heading out
to the April catch.

For now, we may pick a place on any coast,
for we have been given permission
to watch the square, white sails of early galleons

—the liquid rhythm in the naked backs
of their oarsmen-slaves, their only maps
the horizon they must follow
and the horizons left behind.

Gravid

The morning rush of the breath brings
you to these places, puts you in the mood.
What will happen today? Same as yesterday
but late by twenty-four hours
as the infinite jest goes, the one on us.
But we have traveled

much further than that. Today I mean:
all the cats are out of the bag
including the big one who waits like a mouse
after cheese. The lump in your throat sags,

says he's not far away, but what is
these days when each thing rhymes with some thing
...but what?
...which is the missing piece of the puzzle

...which lures you out of house and home
like one more addiction with a smile
on its face, posing from a tree branch,
ready to pounce. No getting around it
—the child beggars in the street
vying for larger and more elaborate
carfare, the sirens that keep you up all night:
They are all nuggets in the same sequence:
the penny's worth of thought the world expects
of you, before, without advance notice,
it moves away from you.

This way it pays to be careful
what constructs we place in the bottle with us
before raising the sails...which puts
me in mind of sailing:

Remember the day we spotted the old loggerhead
gravid with eggs, making her way home
through even more gravid waters?
Of course not. You weren't even there.
Neither was I. But she was. She was.

Book Review
For Bella

In the last chapter attempts are made
to restore a sense of order,
            explain...justify at least. A veil
falls like a small-rain through a white pine forest.
            Tiny gaps of neglect and concern
mingle together about the forest floor.
            Nothing has been purposely omitted
nor made purposely unclear, yet the veil lingers
            beyond the closing sentences.

The two main characters are seated on a flat rock
            at the edge of a pond. They do not speak
or touch. Their feet dangle in the water.
It is a moment of plants. Moss softens
            the air, takes the edge off sharply ascending
            and descending surfaces—gossamer and lace-

like ferns...and the flowering plants: bromeliads,
            pink blossom of peach, thistle, wild rose
grow, wither and pass on their seed. And yet

the two remain seated—no longer mind but sight
—pure vision—they hear the history of plants
            stored in thc moment, their feet
motionless in the water as at that specific season
of the sun when the great loggerheads
            and green sea turtles gravid with eggs
return to the sand from which they emerged

and one more generation of river eels turns
            to return to the Sargasso Sea. They
hear the life of ponds, of plants. They do not speak
            yet their feet linger in the water.

Mayan Tongues

Did you ever pull a poem
out of another poem—breach-wise,
in other words, ass-wise(?)—
kicking, wordless and screaming
—like being on the Battlestar Galactica
now taking place on Star Trek or Wars
and suddenly

your poem is, like, a cylone(?)
or a corpuscle in a boxy Borg empire, one
thing always slipping into the next
like a Mayan painting of a serpent tongue
becoming two heads, one poem into another
taking on putting off love affairs—one undefined

yen to become a politician, followed
by an obsession to win or to be always losing(?)
as though your veins were no longer able
to contain the traffic(?) of clogging platelets
and red blood corpuscles like couriers
of oxygen, gossip and other nutrients
to villages of nerves and hamlets of muscles
and, riding shotgun, white blood corpuscles
against the gangs of attacking viral
and bacterial bandits(?)

as though your heart were about to burst
as in that movie about exploding heads
exploded by larger and more thoughtless alien heads

only this time it's words(?) like on Old McDonald's
farm: here a word, there a word
everywhere a word-word, but no rhythm
no syntax? like a baby-made disaster
leaking through the baby's diaper and mother

comes to the rescue asking what's the matter?
like in a John Berryman dream sequence
in which it is César Vallejo, pried
open to the bone, who said it best
or like the shock to the head
of the shotgun blast, exposing the brain
and closing the mind, while the body lay
for days or weeks, feast of white larvae
becoming blue-bottle flies
and still no word? on how

the schedule of the day is shaping up
for the expelled and expurgated ghost
who has turned the last page of the novel,
waiting for a bus? and, yes, I

remember, yes, while fishing for trout
from a distant galleon, who said
though now it's another voice, and
another one is taking the rap(?)

so, seriously, did it ever happen
that you pulled a poem ass-wise
from someone else's hat? all screaming
and writhing? and it didn't matter(?)
or this is the matter?

Based on True Stories
For Richard Martin, poet

Reading self in the poems of other poets
Reading it back into self's own words
Who goes there? Ghost in the lantern:
"Peg o' my heart

(peg through my heart
and fangs of yearnings past)

       White Fang took
the high road over the hills and through
the woods to head off Little Lonely Cowboy
at the pass. They parted (it was part
of growing up) mid Virgin White Pines
on a ridge in Western, PA

and kind words, but the words
like "kindness," "heaviness," "Brother"
got in the way of what there was to say.

Say, once passions ranged so freely
across the alleys and prairies, my pen
burned holes into the paper, like

the manholes running down
the middle of a street where
the city's nerves and entrails live
topped with manhole covers forged
in India The Old Fashion Way:
slave labor—whole men slowly
melted into the steal. But here

it's only sun when it's not raining
and the little specks of sunlight growing
in your skin are carcinomas, so
I grew old, I grew old

but how old really? Old Man,
there's a place for you, but
this place is no place for old men.

Fairy Tale

By then all time was run out
and the weekly tennis match ran
over the abyssal plain where little
Hanse had laid down the last
of his golden buttons.
It was *pater noster* who

bet the last of the family's heresies
on a shoe-in for the Triple Crown. The rest
was all pastels and a watercolor sky...
up to a point, we might call
a "certain point" but there, again,
language failed to do it justice.

A sure thing
was the daily commute of the arthritis
to my picking finger. Not one to complain, I
buried the dead oriole in the family plot.
We were all grateful for his song.
A weight had been lifted and we
were all happy for that and for

night too where stars pointed
a way, but not how to get there.
I had packed a bag just in case.
My dear Grete was busy
as ever baking "bread" in the oven
she'd acquired. No one
would have guessed what head if
any head had been sent rolling in
the grass before her. We waited
for the birds who'd be back at dawn
to steal our sustenance from the mulberry
bush.

There were ashes
many ashes and falling down,
much falling down.

Old Brooklyn
For John and Carmella

We'd been up and down
that rusty road you'd hardly know
if not for wear: infinite chaos

of summer spewing from the dregs
to the top of prison our bottle, beating time
from behind brown park's hedges
where wild oaks of the mind trembled to life
—their age being anyone's guess, no sense
or science on the agenda that day—

there, only to keep their wooden field static
and trembling, hold back the flood for a while,
so to speak. We,

on the other hand, took turns being ourselves
and each other's dream wraith according to rules
of the unfolding game. I,

for one, hoped to live on a miniature farm
in a locomotive under a pine
at the end of the road, upon
the outset of winter, but

was content to haunt the empty stables
smelling of absent horses and hay,
the sheds where the ice and milk wagons had
been kept in the abandoned Borough
of the lost City. And

stalking the wee gone ones became child's play
while the deer and the antelope played, and
stocks of pigeons—flights, tumblers,
electric blues filled
the iridescent air...

the wine fermenting slowly
in the secret cellars of the ghost men.
My hands, you know, didn't always look
this way, all knotty and gnarly and brittle
as dead leaves. After a morning of hunting
and gathering, dodging busses and trollies,
crossing at the green and in between,
they shone
—blue rays shooting from my fingers.
No one understood us.
I'm sure you remember.
We were all there.
We were a theory of order in chaos,
—electrons in a field—

carving longhorn bison, cave bears,
and panthers seen in magazines

and our names into the bitumen
covered wall of dusty sheds
of the lost City, the abandoned Borough.

Happy Trails

Meantime as all the sheaves of hay
at Bull Barn Curve are spun to gold without
a name or care... there'll be no need for night
and sleep, the dream rises daily
at any given hour and as many times as we may
lower ourselves on this rope

from the gleaming roof beams of desire.
Now all the seasonal washes of the desert
landscape, say cosmos, run with maternal milk.
They are

for you, cowpoke, your palms turned
to honest leather in the roping of these cattle
grazing in the no-time before their appointed
designation, your face a brown pearl in the sun,
your ten-gallon hat, your diaper.

What rises now in the east at the dead
of night through the chinks of yonder window
is the name of all things for the moment,
as lustrous as the nickel plating of the cap
gun at your side. Rise too, cowpoke,

your wish, your virtual palomino,
your rawhide lasso.

In the Interim

have I been good to you this morning,
served you toast, and coffee
in your favorite goblet? And last night
simple sleep...no need to answer
to other needs—yours or mine.

Grandpa was up all night
pacing the floor—where
the attic used to be—
counting his children
(the garden is now a pool)

First, Angela. No. First came
Giuseppe, who died one night
hardly born in his crib. After that,
we were all American. One, maybe,
two who still remember in a language
we no longer understand. But

for now, are we well served:
eggs scrambled...fruit...and the
tiny nuggets of ham, like nuggets
the taste of water in dry sand
....are we served?

No? We don't know? The counting
continues, through morning and midday
to midnight...dainty nuggets of sorrow
exceed, have kept us from sleep.

They forget the who and the where
they are too (the why
is never a question) hidden under cars
behind the trees lining the school yard
and playground, in the hollows
where the traceries were—corpse
and executioner alike—.

In the interim
the coffee is still warm.
May I kiss your forehead,
place my fingers on the wound
to see if it has healed,
to see if you are there.

Falls Away

You wake one morning
and the birds have stopped calling
—nests vacant, nestlings fledged
and gone.

More memory than substance a sense
of empty fields is palatable.
The silence is a chorus
of departed sound.

Like whole notes of a music score
the earth's thesaurus of starlings, grackles
and their kin line up
on overhead wires waiting
for the concert only they will hear
to begin.

How much time is one morning?
How much goes by saying space
into its many crevices and turnings
—fabric of hacked parts, random pieces
and the sudden though not surprising
ending?

If you had wings, you'd hear the music now.
Nothing left to think about.
Your greatest poem
has been written

THE APPROACHING STORM

I

You stumble onto a safe-place. The world
opens to the secret language
                of ferns...lichens
clinging to tree limbs coming to slow
                endings—more sleep
                        than end
more dream than sleep   to make room
                for new positionings, new purposes,
                        new ends

with the sudden croaking of toads
aroused from late summer stasis—the sleepless
                half-life of amphibians—by swells of rain
resurrecting in them the inevitable urge
                to mate: proliferation.

How to read it all, absorb into words
                anticipation kindled by memory
                        of distant thunder
as it threatens to be a storm? Yet
as if shot from one precarious middle-ground
you have stumbled into another:
                the same green tapestry stretched
out before you tentatively across an endless loom:

these new and same live and water oaks
entwining their branches as far as the mind's eye sees
into calligraphies of struggle—vegetable triumph
                failure
mitigated as if through an inherent
                kindness
                        of Spanish moss
the sway of palm, aroma of slash pine.

II

Early this morning, I take my coffee
to the enclosed porch to watch the growing
agitations of wind through the oaks
                rustling the Spanish moss:

a fawn
            emerging from the gallery of trees
yet still half-hidden in the underbrush
            its footsteps tentative
held us
                —for you were there too—in its gaze

as if to question our presence
or the faint scents and signs permeating the air
anticipating the change of weather

affirming its own delicately balanced life
                now in memory confirmed:
                        eternity in our mutual gaze
                                clock in our ticking hearts.

And despite the distance travelled
            —our travail so to speak—our trial—we are joined
in the gaze of this singular wild creature

we are amazed at the urgency of toads
            and the sky as it darkens
to contain the approaching storm.

Yet it is the pronoun itself, this "we":
its sudden persistence as if from nowhere or nothing
yet there and in no rhetorical sense
            —I have not travailed/traveled alone—

in Kichwa even as in Chinese
            it is the pluralized "I"
            word, sound, conflation of beings

yet remaining two separate beings
        that appear as if born from a syntax
          auguring future, growth
on a whim, on a breeze so to speak

or hidden in the language of trees
          and the Spanish moss
now rustling more in the pervasive
signs, this murmur of leaves:

a "you" written into the equation
by no means hypothetical—but there
          all the time—secret sharer
—even to the possessor of the secret:

mutual configurations
        even at great distance
           —turn matching turn
             spin matching spin:

precise integer completing the equation
whose safety is entrusted to the "I"
who promises the same safety
          fragile though it be...
the "we" now emerging
      neither rhetorical or hypothetical
        tentative though it be
          as the hoof-falls
of a fawn.

III

There is more. So little.
What follows will follow in ways
we know almost nothing about: intimacies
of toads play themselves out as we watch
        from the porch
          of the safe-house

we've come upon
as one makes its way haphazardly
to a drainpipe which carries heavier
and heavier flows of rain
                    which the ground can no longer absorb
                    and a puddle appears.

There are toads such is the design
of their species who need only a puddle
lasting long enough for a quick coupling
                    eggs laid
                              sperm released:
metamorphosis from tadpole to toad
                    —matter of days or weeks—
in patterns of proliferation.

I share this story with you:
a gift so small, the meaning barely fits
has all but been lost in the haste
of preparing for our flight

                    something surely
                              will have been
                                        has been forgotten.

For now we have only our hands reaching out
like blind antennae, yours, mine—random
thoughts, remembrances clutter our heads
like the wind-blown twigs and Spanish moss
which now clutter the lawn—

a sudden calm
as if fixed in the gaze of a dreamless sleep.

We are here. The storm carries signs
                    furious
                              in their configuration.

We have ice to keep food fresh, fuel
                for the generator. We have words.
                      We speak.

Nicanor Parra: Anti-Poet/Language Poet

I think I'm ready for that long
poem on sharecropping and other
natural disasters, having

come to regret my earlier remarks
about that piece of paper Nicanor Parra
titled "Graffiti Written on the Mausoleum
of Ezra Pound" and covered with
bi-and-maybe-trilingual graffiti.

Thus,
I still remember the one about
the guy who runs from his home
in search of a "médico" to save
his moribund "mamá" and finds
a pack of cigarettes generations
of fearless men have abandoned
wife, kids, house and home
in search of (though I may have
enhanced here, left a syllable out
there).

They don't make that like them
anymore. I mean a cell phone
could have taken a picture
and saved a thousand words...
and as many pages, and maybe

a sports arena, sunk
like an umbilicus
in the center of Chile,
a thin, terse country,
a long graffito
down the mappa mundi.

One More Time Around

For John Salvatore and Jen Benvenuto

Slowly,
      like the face of your computer
—not this one but the other— things
come to the light. You have been here
before. The marching band

has taken the field, is tuning up,
playing that one chord over and over
—what is it? And suddenly you know
as if all the electrons on the screen
have found their orbit. The majorettes

are twirling and tossing each other
in the air. The whole town—and
the long ago block party
in the secret ward
of the forgotten city— is hoping it won't rain
on this parade and all the games
to follow. And

the one whose teeth shone like stars
through the cloud drift and lost hearts;
she is the one in pink and blue spangles.

No matter. The hospital called
early this morning to sound the all clear
Groceries have been stockpiled
against the coming electrical storms

and the note
left of the kitchen table
for all the late-risers to see
explains everything...
and how to get there.
You are one of the lucky few

to have been chosen. You may now search for
the footsteps of the greats who have come
before you: the survivors and the lost ones.

Their names are engraved
if not in lights then in all
the ensuing dreams that continue

—like a circle or circus.
The marching girls are ready.
The band is tuned.
The music has begun.

Nearly Ghost

Like the one perceived —young man? old woman?—
at the corner of the eye
and only for an instant   who

passes by splashing in the ripples
ending at beach end

or a break in the clouds after a long season
of frustrated rain, and how the crowds
of bystanders screw yellow, blue and red umbrellas
into the sand, smooth the folds and creases
from their blankets

or buy drinks from one of the many concessions
lined up just beyond the road —golds
and bronzes shooting from their bodies
as the sun sets all about them, and as

the light in a far away waiting room
flickers yet a quiet peace
settles into a corner

or we who are all but not here anymore,
have all but disappeared, and how
trope signs to trope, crisis upon crisis,
metaphor at the corner of each street
crossing.

Last Avant-Guard
for John Miller, poet

A vast book it was you gave me,
gravid with secret corridors, lives of the saints
and not, novel ideas, pictures, even, and blank
pages to ponder like certain persons,
each essential in its own way,

lost at street corners among books
and history and doldrums:
ellipses threatening the world with meaning. I read
it from cover to cover, admiring more
and more your courage and indecision;
for, indeed, I was about and among
the same themes, which puts me in mind
of the purpose of the book,

which I believe was your intention:
to feel like a missionary myself and us
on a crusade to save the street children
with their tin cups, and we among them.
But I was going away

you would remain, or was it
the other way around? Game of
hopscotch. These things happen

like a snake sloughing off her skin
and being a new snake. They used skin
—well, parchment—to write books on.
They were the designated vessels, waiting
—nostalgia and misgiving in their sails—
for the voyage to commence: time, place,
port-of-call;

yet once on the immaculate sea
who could have guessed what from whom?

Aya Uma: Spirit Face

(The *Aya Uma* of spirit face is
worn by the leader of a communal
dance celebrating the solstice
in the Andes of Ecuador)

We are in the presence of the Great Thought
—if only we could devise the software,
program to the last punctuation mark
(as for me I think only in the early morning
and only in small doses)

—Ask the Great Thought as it passes by
if it is *Trout Fishing in America*
Love Calls Us to the Things of this World
Poemas Humanos or dawn at the heart
of Mount Imbabura Apu
and, yes, it is
—and process

—for the Great Thought lives in openly
secret places like a thing touched by longing
fathoms deep and away from us always
away yet there changing arctic to summer season
and back —geographic, geologic, pelagic
—never finished or started —in need-of

—escaping-from this or that gloss, footnote
or ruling from a judge's bench   —to pick up
the thread once more and off to the races
(as the saying goes)
—its many ponies and jockeys each with
his or her eyes on the prize
and where it will end —but

it never ends and goes on without them
(ponies and jockeys) hails down a taxi
on 14th St and 2nd Avenue —Spring

108

breeze forever through his or her hair —is
a juggler or minstrel on a street or mountain path
(referred to as *Capac ~Nan*: the "Old Path"
"Ancestor Path") —is

a mountain fox (El Zorro de Arriba)
dressed in parody or paradox: a clown
—sad clown happy clown leading
the procession of drunken dancers
—face to the future —face to the past
as they dance in a circle ever progressing

to a hollow in the hills to a spring in the hollow
where they are cleansed

—That last night
we sit drinking, chatting, texting,
laughing, glossing, longing

—Masks all lying in a corner
lingering in a corner   stir
and off they go one to one
on their own —with us
and without us.

Gloss on "The Sumptuous Hills of Gulfport"

Except for the wind and random breeze from the Gulf
which bring the crests, depressions and occasional whitecap
to the waves of Boca Ciega—mitigated as they are
by the outer peninsula and islands, littered with high-rise
condos and mansions—and not counting the voyageless sailors

who man the homeless sloops, vagrant ketches and yawls
anchored a dozen or so yards into the grassy bay waters, or
the occasional manatee eating the grass and the pod
of all-seasonal dolphins and the group of middle-aged women
twirling old remembrances and hula-hoops around

their waists in exercise groups at the beach, and save for
the ancient scrivener or painter, and the ups and downs
of couples walking their half-blind Labrador or cocky Pomeranian
and the bungalows—some of which have seen
better days and others waiting silently under new

leases and renovation—and excepting the alleys between them
where nature-restored confirms itself, and the cobblestone
streets with occasional cracks and puddles from which
the remnants of palms are lodged, and the male
anoles asserting their right to mate and growth...

there are no sumptuous hills at Gulfport, only
the flight of pelicans, skimmers at rest in the sand,
as if the purpose of life were merely to be more life,
mindless, innocent, unsolicited: a mere rise
and dip of this random moment that surrounds us.

www.ingramcontent.com/pod-product-compliance
Lightning Source LLC
Chambersburg PA
CBHW022034090426
42741CB00007B/1060